The Rewards of the Secret Place

Prayer That Releases the Miraculous

Ian Christensen

malcolm down
PUBLISHING

First published 2010 by Integrity Media Europe
This edition published 2016 by Malcolm Down Publishing Ltd.

www.malcolmdown.co.uk

ISBN 978-1-910786-51-2

Printed in the United Kingdom

Contents

Dedication and Acknowledgements

I dedicate this book to all who are seeking more of God's presence and power in their lives.

A big thank you to my beloved Dennise, and family for releasing me to go away and write. I very much appreciate all the saints at New Life who prayed. And a special acknowledgement to Adam Kucharski who assisted me, working tirelessly on the manuscript.

May God use this book for His greater glory.

Preface

I had been travelling and teaching on the subject of prayer and spiritual warfare for more than two decades. Suddenly, to my surprise, I was receiving fresh insight and revelation from the Lord on a subject with which I was so familiar.

The year was 2007 and I had recently returned from visiting the International House of Prayer in Kansas City, USA. Psalm 91 opened up to me as never before and I began to receive a download of revelation from the Lord.

I had written a book on prayer which was first published in 1991. This book had been used by the Lord to teach people how to develop a strong and consistent prayer life. But now, as I read Psalm 91 over and over again, I began to realise that, as a pastor/preacher and Bible School lecturer, I had never ever taught on Psalm 91 in more than 25 years of ministry. I had taught and touched on so many themes and subjects over the years, but never on Psalm 91.

As I began to develop a teaching series for our local church and our weekly television programme, I observed anew the significance of verse 1 of this Psalm:

"He who dwells in the secret place of the Most High shall abide under the shadow of the Almighty."

As my eyes were being opened by the Lord I saw afresh where the "secret place" is. The Lord was showing me how we can encounter Father God again and again in this "secret place". I began to discover not only *where* the secret place is but also *what we do* in it, and I realised that there are rewards – yes, *great* rewards! – for those who dwell in it. What is this secret place? It is a place of intimacy, a place of encounter, a place where we are refreshed and a place from where the miraculous is released in great measure in and through our lives.

I also felt very strongly that I was being given a message for the body of Christ worldwide, as part of the preparation for the return of our Lord and Saviour, as He returns for His Bride, the Church.

Let's discover together, in the pages of this book, *the rewards of the secret place.*

Foreword

The Rewards of the Secret Place is a compelling invitation into a life of intimate communion with the Father through dynamic personal prayer. Writing from his own extensive and profound experience as a man of prayer, Ian Christensen has given us a biblically-based vision of the abiding fruit that grows from the soil of our secret times with the Father.

This book, rooted in the teaching of Jesus in the Sermon on the Mount, is an accessible and un-intimidating description of the power of prayer and a passionate rallying cry to the body of Christ to prioritise the practice of round-the-clock worship and intercession today. Speaking for myself, it stirred an intense hunger to go deeper and further in my private prayer times. I recommend this book to all believers – especially those who need help cultivating their alone times with Abba Father.

Dr Mark Stibbe
Author and Founder/CEO of
Kingdom Writing Solutions

Foreword

The Rewards of the Secret Place is a simple, yet comprehensive teaching book that reveals to readers exactly what the title conveys. I write as someone who has personally benefited from the writer's deep knowledge and experience of intimacy with God, and can bear testimony to the truths contained within these pages.

Ian Christensen writes from the perspective of having *lived in* the truths contained in this book, and for that reason you feel the weight and richness of the truths he communicates in each chapter. But the real benefit of this book is realised when one begins to enjoy for oneself the reality of those truths.

I am privileged to know the author and have no hesitation in recommending this book to every Christian who is serious about getting to know God better, as well as those whose desire to see an increase in the miraculous power of God working in their lives.

John Partington
National Leader,
Assemblies of God, Great Britain

What others are saying about this book

Ian Christensen is undoubtedly a man in pursuit of a life of prayer. From the lessons he and his wife have learned over the years he will take you on a journey to a place of supernatural power, produced through a life of prayer. Ian has successfully opened up in this excellent book the strategic place of intimacy in our life with the Father and the keys and results of abiding there. A recommended read for all those who long for God's power to be released upon a lost and dying world.

Ken Gott
Senior Leader,
Bethshan Church, Newcastle

In a busy world, prayer is often sacrificed to the detriment of the individual believer's and therefore the church's effectiveness. In his book Ian brings us a sharp reminder of the importance of prayer, but he has also written with inspiration to encourage us to experience a transformed life of intimacy with God. Ian's is a practitioner of what he writes. I am very happy to recommend this fine book.

Paul Weaver
Former Superintendent,
Assemblies of God, Great Britain and Ireland

E.M. Bounds wrote, "Preaching is not the performance of an hour, it is the outflow of a life. It takes twenty years to make a sermon, because it takes twenty years to make the man. The true sermon is a thing of life. The sermon grows because the man grows. The sermon is forceful because the man is forceful. The sermon is holy because the man is holy. The sermon is full of the divine unction because the man is full of the divine unction."

I believe Ian Christensen is such a man – a person of integrity who who practices what he preaches and writes. He is a man of prayer and a man of the Word. This adds power, weight and authenticity to his message. This book contains a "now" word for the body of Christ. I pray we will hear what the Holy Spirit is saying to the Church at this time. Abiding in the secret place will anchor us in the reality of the unseen, eternal realm of Heaven. This changes everything about the way we perceive and live in the temporal (or temporary) realm. People who abide with Christ in the secret place learn to pull the realities of the eternal realm into this temporal realm. Jesus is our high example of this. The Father is presently raising up multiplied thousands who will manifest Heaven on Earth. Living in the secret place is essential to this happening.

This book will inspire and motivate you, but also give you practical keys to begin your journey into the secret place of the Most High. I highly recommend it.

Steve Uppal
Senior Leader,
All Nations Christian Centre, Wolverhampton

In this new book Ian has hit another home run! The delicious secret in this book is that actually, there is no secret! The rewards of consistent daily devotion, sustained, heartfelt and biblically-informed intercession are available to anyone who wants to have them. The demonstrated humility of a Christian who makes a daily, intentional appointment to meet with God will be rewarded in remarkable ways. I salute Ian for presenting these truths in a such an engaging and uncluttered way. Read the book and on your way to the "secret place" give a copy to a friend!

Doug Williams
Senior Pastor,
Emmanuel Christian Centre, Walthamstow

CHAPTER 1

A Personal Testimony

Learning the benefits of prayer ...

It seems as if God has always been speaking to me about prayer. When I first became a Christian I was challenged by a book I read to spend an hour a day in prayer.

The year was 1975 and I had just married my beautiful bride, Dennise. We lived in a small, one-bedroom flat, and at the time I was definitely not a morning person. I vividly remember my first attempts to establish a daily prayer time. Getting up early was not an option in those days. Oh no!

I would go into our sitting room with my Bible and, as instructed by the book, spend 15-20 minutes in prayer and Bible reading as I worked my way up to the 60 minutes. As I persisted day after day into the night, attempting to spend an hour with God, I was frequently awakened by the noise of my own snoring! Oh dear! What would I do? I did, however, persist in my efforts and, after several weeks, I was spending an hour a day with the Lord. I prayed at night and when I awoke in the morning I said a quick prayer and made my way to work.

As I began to establish this discipline in my life, I noticed some remarkable changes in my demeanour. I had more faith and confidence in my God, I witnessed more effectively to people at work, and I just felt so much stronger in my everyday Christian walk with God. At this point in my Christian journey I was not familiar with the words of Matthew 26:40-41:

"Then He came to the disciples and found them sleeping, and said to Peter, 'What! Could you not watch with Me one hour? Watch and pray, lest you enter into temptation. The spirit indeed is willing, but the flesh is weak.'"

I enjoyed the benefits of my daily time with the Lord but, as time progressed and Angela, our first daughter, came along in October 1976, the everyday pressures of work, family, church and leisure gradually squeezed out my daily prayer time. Personal prayer was now hurried, fitted in where possible, and Bible reading became intermittent and irregular. Little did I realise at the time that millions and millions of Christians around the world were encountering similar problems in attempting to establish a daily devotional time with the Lord.

No one had taught me *why* it was important to pray. I did not know the benefits of prayer and certainly did not understand what happens when we spend quality time with the Lord, and equally, what *does not* happen when we neglect to spend time alone with Him.

I love the following quote by Paul Yonggi Cho:

"God has created us in such a way that we need to understand the purpose and the benefit of something if we are going to be motivated to do it."

I did not understand the benefits of prayer, which are many. So I went to church, went to work, enjoyed my family, and prayed and read the Bible alone occasionally when I could. I was a serious Christian, intent on following the Lord, belonging to a church, and I was hungry for fellowship and Bible knowledge. Spending an hour with the Lord daily, however, was now a forgotten decision.

I was so hungry for more of the Lord and so longed to know my Bible better that I enrolled in Christian Life College under

Jean and Elmer Darnall in 1977. As I studied one of the subjects, Prayer and Intercession (as taught by Jean), my passion and desire for prayer was gradually rekindled. I remember getting top marks in my exam and I graduated from Christian Life College in 1979 older and wiser, and with an increased knowledge of the Bible.

After graduating I felt called by the Lord to fast for 21 days, eating one light meal a day. I was familiar with fasting, but felt impressed by the Lord to fast and pray in this way while continuing in my job, working for the Department of Employment in Wembley, England. Shortly after this fast I was invited to pastor a church in Wembley.

Dennise and I moved to our new church and I became the Pastor of Wembley Assemblies of God Church in January 1980. Our second child, John, was born in August of that year and, on the night of his birth, while Dennise was still in hospital, I felt the Lord speak to me at midnight. I wrote down what I felt the Lord was saying. He said that I was called to be the pastor of this church and that in time we would see many signs and wonders and miracles, so much so that the television cameras and the newspapers would come to see what was happening in our midst.

In 1982 our third child, Sarah, was born, and we were now a family of five. Our church was small: there were twelve adults when we took it over, and now, as 1982 went into 1983, we had about 30-40 people in the fellowship. Although many aspects of church life were good, it was amazing how much pressure a small church could generate.

By 1983 I was feeling very discouraged and was seriously considering resignation. I was saved by a word of knowledge from an American preacher named Dan Sneed at a Full Gospel Businessmen's Fellowship International dinner. Dan picked me out of the crowd, even though he did not know me, and said that God was saying that I was to stay where I was because He had plans to do great things there. The word was very timely and encouraging. Dan also said a few other things that confirmed what God had spoken to me in the past.

During this whole period I prayed. They say everybody prays, even people who don't profess to believe in God seem to pray instinctively in a crisis! I prayed and read my Bible and prepared sermons and led prayer meetings like every other minister. However, as I look back, something was missing. I prayed in desperation, in a crisis, and prayed like most Christians and ministers do, but without any clear revelation as to the purpose of prayer. I did not fully understand the whys and the wherefores of prayer, and so we saw a few things happen here and there – a few people were saved, filled with the Holy Spirit, taught and encouraged – but everything we were seeing seemed measured and small.

Around 1983/84 my good friend, Doug Williams (whom I had met at Christian Life College), came to join me in the ministry. We prayed together often when Doug was on the staff, and part of his job description was to pray for two and a half hours daily, an hour of which was to be for me and my family.

Then things began to improve and our church began to grow, and during this period we renamed it New Life Christian Centre. Between 1980 and 1986 we had two church splits and our membership fluctuated up and down as a consequence.

During this time I felt that the Lord had put me in an enclosure and kept speaking to me about personal and corporate prayer in so many different ways. There were several books and a few key people who influenced me during this period, but I felt the Lord teaching me about prayer, intercession and spiritual warfare.

There were many key lessons to learn and I was slowly beginning to understand the place of prayer, why it is necessary, what happens in and through prayer, and what *does not happen* when prayer is absent.

"Unless we learn to pray, we become a prey."

(Unknown)

CHAPTER 2

More Prayer - More Power

No man is greater than his prayer life ...

I believe that there is a distinct connection between prayer and the miraculous. A great man of God was once asked, "How is it that, whenever you preach, *the power of the Holy Spirit is present?*" His answer was quite simple, but profound. He said, "Much prayer, much power; little prayer, little power; no prayer ..." and he smiled.

Here is a quotation from Leonard Ravenhill:

"No man is greater than his prayer life. The pastor who is not praying is playing, the people who are not praying are straying. We have many organisers but few agonisers; many players and payers, but few prayers; many singers, few clingers; lots of pastors, few wrestlers; many fears, few tears; much fashion, little passion; many interferers, few intercessors; many writers but few fighters.

Failing here, we fail everywhere."

Dr Derek Prince said:

"Prayer is the generator that keeps all the fittings in the building working."

Matthew 21:1-16 is a very powerful passage. Here Jesus is on His way to Jerusalem. He sends two of His disciples to fetch Him a donkey. Jesus knows what the donkey is for, but the disciples simply obey and go out to fetch the donkey. As they collect the donkey and her colt we are told (v4) that this is a fulfilment of Zechariah's prophecy (v5):

> *"Tell the daughter of Zion,*
> *'Behold your King is coming to you,*
> *lowly and sitting on a donkey,*
> *a colt, the foal of a donkey.'"*

As Jesus enters Jerusalem, He receives a tremendous welcome:

> *"A very great multitude spread their clothes on the road . . .*
> *The multitudes . . . cried out, saying 'Hosanna to the Son of*
> *David' . . . All the city was moved . . .*

and proclaimed Him as,

> *. . . the prophet from Nazareth of Galilee."* (v8-11)

The Lord Jesus never had a day like this before or after this incident. This was His time of maximum popularity. With the eyes of the whole city on Him (v10), this was an excellent time for Jesus to make a statement that He wanted all to hear.

With the whole city hanging on His every word and action, Jesus carries out one of the most profound and important acts of His ministry.

As He enters the temple area, Jesus drives out those engaging in other activities. He shouts loud and clear:

> *"It is written, 'My house shall be called a house of prayer,'*
> *but you have made it a 'den of thieves.'"* (v13)

Jesus is visibly upset as He sees a place where people should be praying and worshipping used for other activities. He immediately expresses His disgust and *rearranges the furniture to accommodate prayer*. I believe that Jesus would like to rearrange the furniture in our lives and in our churches to accommodate prayer.

As I have taught on prayer across this nation and in many nations of the world for over twenty years now, I have found prayer to be very lacking in the lives of Christians. Most Christians, possibly more than 95%, do not have a daily encounter with God on a regular basis. But when we begin to seek God daily and regularly, *everything begins to change for the better.*

One of my favourite scriptures is Psalm 34:10:

"The young lions lack and suffer hunger, but those who seek the LORD shall not lack any good thing."

Here is another quotation from Leonard Ravenhill:

"The tragedy of this late hour is that we have too many dead men in the pulpit giving out too many dead sermons to too many dead people. Preaching without unction kills instead of giving life. A sermon born in the head reaches the head; a sermon born in the heart reaches the heart. Yet ministers who do not spend two hours a day in prayer are not worth a dime a dozen, degree or no degree. Away with palsied, powerless preaching, which is unmoving because it was born in a tomb instead of a womb and nourished in a fireless, prayerless soul. We may preach and perish, but we can't pray and perish."

The truth of the matter is that prayer is by far the most spiritual, the most taxing and exacting work that a man can engage in. Meanwhile, *"theology without kneeology issues in pathology"* (a quote from *Prayer Generals*).

We go on to read in Matthew 21:14:

"Then the blind and the lame came to Him in the temple, and He healed them."

Once the place had been cleared for prayer and the furniture rearranged to accommodate prayer, then the miraculous flowed.

There is a distinct connection between abundant prayer and the miraculous.

I see three places that are meant to be houses of prayer:

1. Our bodies are the temple of the Holy Spirit (1 Corinthians 3:16). We need to become houses of prayer. There is so much more that could be said about this.

2. Our homes should be houses of prayer.

3. Our churches are meant to become houses of prayer.

In effect, Jesus was saying, "If it's *My* house, then it needs to be a house of prayer." And a house of prayer naturally becomes a house of miracles.

In about 2001 I was in a meeting in Marsham Street near Westminster Abbey. I received a prophetic word from a well-known prophet that our church in Wembley would become a 24/7 house of prayer.

We began our house of prayer in August 2007 with just two hours a day. At present, after visiting two 24/7 houses of prayer, we now pray around 70 hours per week. Our goal is 168 hours per week, but we have noticed the increase of God's presence and power in our midst.

There is so much more to share along these lines. God has given me a passion to promote and mobilise and motivate people and churches to pray.

I believe the man of God was right: "Much prayer, much power; little prayer, little power; no prayer, no power."

"God has created us in such a way that we need to know the purpose and benefit of something if we are going to be motivated to work for that thing."

(Dr Paul Yonggi Cho)

CHAPTER 3

The Benefits of Prayer

Prayer is multi-faceted...

In chapter 1 I mentioned how different I felt as I began to spend an hour a day with God. Although initially it was a battle, once established I would describe it as "feeling born again all over again".

Often people undersell prayer. They say prayer is simply talking to God or prayer is talking to God and listening to Him. But prayer is multifarious – made up of many parts.

Prayer involves and incorporates worship, submission, intimacy, petition, spiritual warfare, self-examination and heart searching, intercession, thanksgiving, fasting and more. Prayer is a huge subject and whole books have been written using some of the above as headings. However, daily prayer can be simple, enjoyable and easy to engage in. We will examine the major daily ingredients of prayer in a later chapter.

1. In prayer we meet God and get to know Him

There is no better way to get to know our God than to spend quality and quantity time with Him each day. I have heard Peter Wagner say,

"Take a quantity of time (one hour) and fill it with quality prayer."

Towards the end of his life, king David stands up in front of all his leaders, advisers and mighty men, and he gives advice to his son Solomon as he is taking over the leadership of God's people:

> *"As for you, my son Solomon,* **know the God of your father,** *and serve Him with a loyal heart and with a willing mind; for the LORD searches all hearts and understands all the intent of the thoughts.* **If you seek Him, He will be found by you;** *but if you forsake Him, He will cast you off forever."* (1 Chronicles 28:9)

Yes, in prayer, alone with Him, we get to know Him and develop intimacy and deepen our relationship with Him.

I don't think that there is anything in our lives which is more important than this.

Jesus said to Martha:

> *"One thing is needed, and Mary has chosen that good part, which will not be taken away from her."* (Luke 10:42)

2. We are strengthened in prayer

Through prayer and God's Word we are strengthened to overcome the world, the flesh and the devil. Consider the following scriptures carefully (Isaiah 40:29-31):

> *"He gives power to the weak,*
> *And to those who have no might He increases strength.*
> *Even the youths shall faint and be weary,*
> *And the young men shall utterly fall,*
> **But those who wait on the LORD**
> **Shall renew their strength;**
> *They shall mount up with wings like eagles,*
> *They shall run and not be weary,*
> *They shall walk and not faint."*

In Luke's Gospel, as Jesus is wrestling in prayer in the garden of Gethsemane (22:39-46), He invites the disciples to join Him in prayer (a fuller account is given in Matthew 26:36-46). The disciples did not join Him in prayer as they kept falling asleep. Hmm! A common problem!

But in verse 43 we are told that an angel came to *strengthen Him*:

> *"Then an angel appeared to Him from heaven, strengthening Him."*

There are many other scriptures that attest to the fact that God strengthens us as we interact with Him in prayer.

3. We receive revelation and direction in prayer

In 1986 I had a vivid dream. In it a man of God came up to me, pointed in my face and said, *"You have not taken time to seek the Lord. You need to take seven days to seek Him."* As he finished speaking I awoke and found myself staring at the ceiling. I instinctively knew that the Lord was calling me to seek Him in seven days of fasting and prayer.

As I lay there in the dark, I asked the Lord to confirm the dream with Scripture (something I often do). Almost immediately I remembered Acts 16:9-10:

> *"And a vision appeared to Paul in the night. A man of Macedonia stood and pleaded with him, saying, 'Come over to Macedonia and help us.' Now after he had seen the vision, immediately we sought to go to Macedonia, concluding that the Lord had called us to preach the gospel to them."*

In response to this instruction I went on a seven day fast in secret, on fruit juices only and, on the sixth night of the fast, the

Lord spoke to me through the most powerful and impacting dream I have had to date. As the dream ended, I awoke and the room was full of His presence. I asked the Lord to interpret the dream and instantly began to see the meaning. I then asked the Lord to confirm the dream with a scripture. Again, almost instantly a scripture flashed into my mind. I checked out the scripture (which confirmed the dream) and made a special note of four things God had spoken to me through the dream. In it God spoke to me about my past, present and future. Some of the dream is yet to be fulfilled and influences my outlook to this very day.

Yes, in and through prayer we can receive revelation and direction for our lives and for the lives of others.

4. Through prayer our faith is quickened

In prayer our faith and the faith of others can be quickened, enlivened and increased. Jesus is called *"the author and finisher of our faith."*

Faith does not only come by hearing the Word of God. It also comes from *being with* the Word of God, Jesus (John 1:1-4).

In Hebrews 12:2 we are told to run this race with endurance,

"looking unto Jesus, the author and finisher of our faith."

Whenever we spend time with Him, our faith is enlarged and quickened.

> *"And the Lord said, 'Simon, Simon! Indeed, Satan has asked for you, that he may sift you as wheat. But I have prayed for you, that your faith should not fail; and when you have returned to Me, strengthen your brethren.'"* (Luke 22:31-32)

Here, Peter's faith is strengthened through Jesus' prayer. We too can pray in the same way, for others.

5. Through prayer we are helped to overcome tempt

Again, in the garden of Gethsemane, Jesus invites His disciples, Peter, James and John, to join Him in prayer. He returns to them several times, only to find them sleeping.

> *"Then He came to the disciples and found them asleep, and said to Peter, 'What! Could you not watch with Me one hour? Watch and pray, lest you enter into temptation. The spirit indeed is willing, but the flesh is weak."* (Matthew 26:40-41)

The disciples didn't "watch and pray" and subsequently entered into temptation and ran off and deserted Jesus. Prayer is a spiritual activity. It requires a violent decision and commitment. The flesh is weak and would much rather sleep or watch too much television.

6. Through prayer we receive peace

> *"Be anxious for nothing, but in everything by prayer and supplication, with thanksgiving, let your requests be made known to God; and the peace of God, which surpasses all understanding, will guard your hearts and minds through Christ Jesus."* (Philippians 4:6-7)

The benefits of prayer are many. Through prayer we have victory, provision, power, confidence and more. We neglect prayer at our own peril. God does not legally demand that we pray, but when we do, *we* are the ones who benefit.

*"He shall call upon Me, and I will answer him;
I will be with him in trouble,
I will deliver him and honour him."*

(Psalm 91:15)

CHAPTER 4

What about the Secret Place?

An intimacy and power
beyond the norm ...

As I read Psalm 91 again and again I began to realise that this psalm was speaking about a person who was amazingly blessed by the Lord. The psalmist was not only referring to himself, but also to a "type" of person who was encountering the Lord with great intimacy and supernatural intervention. Look, for example, at verse 7:

> *"A thousand may fall at your side,*
> *and ten thousand at your right hand;*
> *but it shall not come near you."*

I read a true story about two soldiers who were in battle together. They were close friends and in the midst of battle they were isolated and surrounded by the enemy. Realising that if they stayed in their bunker they would be blown up, they decided to come out with guns blazing. As they came up out of the bunker, one of the soldiers was hit by a bullet and fell back to the ground. When the second soldier realised his friend was gone he went crazy, shooting wildly at the enemy. Soon no one was firing back as he had taken out all of those in front of him. He then ran back and opened his friend's uniform to examine the wound. Incredibly, there was no blood as the bullet had hit a Bible in his friend's pocket. He was not dead, only stunned from the fall. When the Bible was examined it was later discovered that the bullet had penetrated so far, but had inexplicably stopped at Psalm 91 and the hole was at verse 7:

> *"A thousand may fall at your side . . . but it shall not come near you."*

The Lord is undoubtedly very good at making His point.

As I continued to examine this psalm it was apparent that the type of person being referred to had an unusually close relationship with the Lord.

> *"I will say of the Lord, 'He is my refuge and my fortress;*
> *My God, in Him I will trust'" . . .*
> *He shall cover you with His feathers,*
> *and under His wings you shall take refuge;*
> *His truth shall be your shield and buckler."* (v2-4)

I understood that Psalm 91 was a popular passage with Christians worldwide and that many of God's people had memorised and used this psalm regularly. I began to ask myself: "Where are the people that experience the reality of this passage? Does this psalm refer to all Christians or are there some conditions involved?" Having pastored and led God's people for more than thirty years, I understand that there are very few who experience this kind of supernatural lifestyle and intervention on a regular basis.

"Who is this psalm referring to?" I asked myself. "Who can enjoy this kind of relationship with the Lord?"

Consider verse 15:

> *"He shall call upon Me, and I will answer him;*
> *I will be with him in trouble*
> *I will deliver him and honour him."*

Also consider:

"Because you have made the Lord, who is my refuge,
  even the Most High, your dwelling place,
no evil shall befall you,
  nor shall any plague come near your dwelling" (v9-10)

and,

"You shall tread upon the lion and the cobra,
  the young lion and the serpent you shall trample underfoot.
Because he has set his love upon Me, therefore I will
  deliver him;
  I will set him on high, because he has known My name."
(v13-14)

Clearly the person spoken about in these lines experiences intimacy and power way beyond what the average Christian experiences. As the Lord opened up this passage, I perceived that the answer was in verse 1:

"He who dwells in the secret place of the Most High shall
  abide under the shadow of the Almighty."

It is the person *"who dwells in the secret place"* who abides under God's shadow that experiences intimacy and a supernatural lifestyle.

Even though I had taught on prayer in churches, conferences and Bible schools, I was beginning to consider afresh what it means to "dwell in the secret place of the Most High".

Psalm 91 speaks of this "secret place" but does not give us any details about where it is or what we do in that place of intimacy. The Lord Jesus, however, *does* tell us where the secret place is and how we should conduct ourselves there. Right in the middle of His Sermon on the Mount, Jesus goes into some detail about the "where" and the "how" of the secret place.

*"But you, when you pray, go into your room,
and when you have shut your door, pray to your Father
who is in the secret place; and your Father who sees
in secret will reward you openly."*

(Matthew 6:6)

CHAPTER 5

What Jesus Taught About the Secret Place

(1)

Approaching the secret place one day at a time...

At present Dennise and I have been pastoring at New Life Christian Centre for just over thirty years. Our wonderful children, Angela, John and Sarah have grown up. Angela is married with two sons, Nathan and Ethan; Sarah is married with two daughters, Kya and Kamea; John is 29 years old and is yet to be married. I'm sure you have seen the car bumper sign which says' "If I knew grandchildren were so much fun, I would have had them first"!

God has wonderfully blessed our church and we have seen significant growth over the years. We have a great team of pastors, elders and leaders, and we have planted several churches at home and abroad. By God's grace our church is known in our area and beyond as a "praying church". Our prayer journey has been long and slow, but we have noticed that as prayer and seeking the Lord increases so also does the working and the power of the Holy Spirit. God answers prayer. God responds to those who seek Him.

There are different levels or places of prayer:

personal prayer
family prayer
church/corporate prayer
inter-church prayer

denominational prayer
national prayer
international prayer (such as the Global Day of Prayer)

God is interested in igniting us at all levels. We are living in a day when, as never before, God is calling His people into the place of prayer, warfare and intercession, so that we can possess the land.

Jesus' teaching on the secret place, right in the middle of His most important teachings in the Sermon on the Mount, must be understood and applied.

Our Lord said,

"When you pray, go into your room and shut the door."

He continues:

"When you have shut the door, *pray to your Father,* **who is in** *'the secret place.'*

Jesus tells us that our Father is there, in that secluded, appointed place, waiting to meet with us. Can you believe that? Jesus said that a room of our own choosing (*"go into* **your** *room and shut the door"*) can be a meeting place with Father God. Jesus calls that designated place, behind a closed door, "the secret place".

It's amazing that God allows us to decide where our "secret place" with Him will be:

> *"But you, when you pray,*
> *go into* **your room,**
> *and when you have shut* **your door,**
> *pray to your Father*
> *who is in the secret place."*

Wow! *We* choose the secret place: a room, *our* room. We enter that room, close the door because it is a place of intimacy and

Father God is there. It sounds incredible, but it's true. I read these verses for years, but never saw this truth so clearly: *"Pray to the Father, who is in the secret place."*

This sheds new light on Psalm 91:1:

> *"He who dwells in the secret place of the Most High . . ."*

The "Most High" is one of the titles of God our Father. Jesus is speaking about the same "secret place" that is being referred to here by the psalmist, promising that the person who lives in this secret place,

> *". . . shall abide under the shadow of the Almighty."*

All the way through Matthew chapter 6, and especially in verses 6-18, Jesus is talking about us interacting with God the Father.

Here is a definition of the secret place:

> The secret place is a place that we go to *every day* to encounter God.
> It is a scheduled, secluded place,
> an isolated place,
> a place kept only for God and ourselves.

You will notice that I said the secret place is an *everyday* experience. Jesus taught this and we will examine this later.

We are daily beings: we live one day at a time. There are several things that we do every day, under normal circumstances:

1. we eat every day
2. we sleep every day
3. we wash and clean ourselves every day

Some of us shave every day, comb our hair every day, unless you have a very wide parting! We are daily beings and we were designed to meet with God every day. Our Lord wants us to meet with Him daily. And as we meet with Him day after day, in that secluded, scheduled place behind the shut door in our room, we are changed forever from glory to glory.

"The secret place is your portal to the throne,
the place where you taste of heaven itself.
Receive this word and you have gained one of the
greatest secrets to intimacy with God."

(Bob Sorge)

CHAPTER 6

Defining the Secret Place

"He who **dwells** in the secret place of the Most High"

(Psalm 91:1a)

We have seen how Jesus emphasises the importance of the secret place. In Psalm 91 the Lord speaks of *dwelling* in the secret place. What does this mean?

To "dwell" means "to reside or abide in a place". It also means "to live . . . to spend one's time . . . to linger . . . to continue long and to delay".

The person who dwells, resides or abides in the secret place has a special place in God's heart. God does not bless us all equally. He loves us all equally, but those who seek Him "find Him". Numerous scriptures confirm this truth:

"Ask, and it will be given to you; seek, and you will find; knock, and it will be opened to you. For everyone who asks receives, and he who seeks finds, and to him who knocks it will be opened." (Matthew 7:7-8)

"And you will seek Me and find Me, when you search for Me with all your heart." (Jeremiah 29:13)

"Then they entered into a covenant to seek the LORD God of their fathers with all their heart and with all their soul; and whoever would not seek the LORD God of Israel was to be put to death, whether small or great, whether man or

woman. Then they took an oath before the LORD *with a loud voice, with shouting and trumpets and rams' horns. And all Judah rejoiced at the oath, for they had sworn with all their heart and sought Him with all their soul; and He was found by them, and the* LORD *gave them rest all around."* (2 Chronicles 15:12-15)

Under King Asa's leadership God's people sought Him and He showed up and blessed them abundantly.

In 2 Chronicles 26:5 it says of King Uzziah that,

> *"He sought God in the days of Zechariah, who had under-standing in the visions of God; and **as long as he sought the*** LORD, **God made him prosper.***"*

Sadly, later on King Uzziah sinned and stopped seeking God and He lost God's blessing on His life.

There are too many scriptures to mention. It is sufficient to say that those who seek the Lord will find Him. The words "dwell" and "abide" have very similar meanings. Like the word "dwell", to abide can mean to "live . . . remain . . . wait . . . continue". Jesus said in John 15:7:

> *"If you abide in Me, and My words abide in you, you will ask what you desire, and it shall be done for you."*

This scripture clearly indicates that there is a place of abiding in God where answered prayer becomes the norm.

James said,

> *"You do not have because you do not ask. You ask and do not receive, because **you ask amiss**, that you may spend it on your pleasures."* (James 4:2b-3)

In the secret place we learn not to pray "amiss", but to pray according to God's will.

"If you abide in Me, and My words abide in you,
will ask what you desire, and it shall be done for y
(John 15:7)

"Now this is the confidence that we have in Him, that if we
ask anything according to His will, He hears us. And if
we know that He hears us, whatever we ask, we know that
we have the petitions that we have asked of Him." (1 John
5:14-15)

We have often heard it said that God always answers prayer –
sometimes He says "yes", sometimes "no" and sometimes "wait".
In the secret place we are taught to pray correctly, so that we
frequently hear the Father saying "yes" or "wait". If we are always
praying and God is constantly having to say "no" to us, then we
are praying out of line with His will and we need to know and
understand His Word better. God has His own timing. When
He keeps us waiting, we simply have to trust Him. Abraham
and Sarah waited, Joseph waited, David waited. Let's get to
know Him and experience John 15:7 instead of James 4:3.

So this is how it works: your dwelling is the place where you
live. You live in a place and from there you go to work, to the
shops, to church and so on. We go from our dwelling place and
return there. You live out of your dwelling place, always returning
to where you live.

Such is the secret place: it is the place from which we live out our
lives. We dwell in the secret place and from there we go out into
our everyday living. We live out of and from the secret place.

The secret place is the beginning, not the end. It is not something
we aspire to reach eventually, it is the foundation from which we
live our lives. Our daily intimacy with the Father sets us up to
become what I call "a Psalm 91 person".

As the Bridegroom prepares to return for His Bride, the
Church, I believe the Body of Christ will increasingly be drawn

into a place of love and intimacy. The secret place is part of Jesus' great preparation of His Bride. The true end time Church that Jesus is building (Matthew 16:18) will be composed of individuals whom the Lord has brought into a place of great closeness and intimacy with Him and dwelling in the secret place is part of His great plan to draw us nearer to Him.

"Satan dreads nothing but prayer. The one concern of the devil is to keep the saints from praying. He fears nothing from prayerless studies, prayerless work, prayerless religion. He laughs at our toils, mocks our wisdom, but he trembles when we pray."

(Samuel Chadwick)

CHAPTER 7

We Can Become a House of Prayer

Making room for intimacy …

I said in chapter 2 that I believe there are three places that are meant to be "houses of prayer":

1. *Ourselves.* As temples of the Holy Spirit we ourselves can become houses of prayer.

2. *Our homes* can become houses of prayer

3. *Our churches* can become houses of prayer

The main focus of this book is to draw us as individuals to become houses of prayer. Jesus is calling His Bride into a place of intimacy with Him and our intimacy is accomplished by spending time in prayer in His presence.

Bob Sorge says, "The greatest warfare always surrounds your prayer life." I have experienced the truth of that comment, haven't you? There is very little opposition to watching the news or the X Factor, or our other favourite programmes, but the moment we decide to make prayer a daily discipline, all of hell seems to come against us.

We currently live in a society where many shops, restaurants and homes openly display idols of other gods. This of course attracts and promotes the working of other spirits that are in opposition to the Kingdom of God.

Our homes need to be houses of prayer where individual and family prayer raises an altar to the Living God. I hate to give the enemy any credit, but he is good at what he does and he has had thousands of years of experience. Satan hates prayer, whether individual, family, church or inter-church prayer. He knows what can happen when people begin to pray and trust God. He also knows what will *not* happen when people are *not* praying.

We have all heard the saying: A family that prays together stays together. However, I would like to highlight *how* we create room for prayer in our homes. The above saying is very general and I have never met a Christian who disagrees with this quote. However, I have met hundreds, possibly thousands of Christians who continually struggle to develop strong individual and corporate prayer lives. Remember, prayer is dependence on God (Luke 18:1).

Firstly, let our homes be places where we individually dwell in the secret place. My first priority after I wake up is to spend time with Him, praying in English, praying in tongues and reading His Word. Dennise and I have three grown children, four grandchildren and two foster children. We have been fostering for nearly ten years and have had more than fifty children in our home.

I wake up in the morning, do the things I have to do and then go into the secret place with Him. My wife Dennise also spends time alone with the Lord before she goes into the day. I have taught all of our children to spend time alone with the Lord each day and I remember the days in the late 80s when most of our rooms had family members praying alone with Him, before entering into the day.

It is good to pray together as a family. Various circumstances often conspire against this, such as an unsaved member or a tricky teenager. It is not easy, but it is essential. If nobody wants to pray in your home, let it start with you. That's how I started.

Sometimes, especially when the children were young, we would pray in the car together on the way to school. Even simply holding hands together and saying the Lord's Prayer is a great place to start.

Mobile prayer units

When Jesus was walking and living on this planet, for the first time God the Father had someone who moved around and prayed and all His prayers were answered. In the same way the Lord needs us to be mobile prayer units, so that wherever we go we pray and things change. We are called to pray for His kingdom to come and for His will to be done on earth.

I understand that there is more to the Christian walk than prayer, but prayer is the beginning, not the end. It is the foundation from which we launch out to do all we do more effectively. Read these two scriptures carefully:

"If you abide in Me, and My words abide in you, you will ask what you desire, and it shall be done for you." (John 15:7)

Notice the word "you" appears five times. The emphasis is very much on us and what we do. We are called to abide in Him and in His word and pray life-changing prayers wherever we go. Here fruitfulness is linked with answered prayer, as Jesus goes on to say:

"By this My Father is glorified, that you bear much fruit; so you will be My disciples." (John 15:8)

Later in this awesome passage Jesus links fruitfulness with answered prayer for a second time. A person who is always praying amiss has not gone very deep with God, but consider this scripture (John 15:16):

*"You did not choose Me, but I chose you and appointed you that you should go and bear fruit, and that your fruit should remain, **that whatever you ask the Father in My name He may give you.**"*

God has chosen, during this dispensation, to work on this earth through our prayers and actions. When we learn to dwell in the secret place we encounter Him, get to know Him, and have the privilege of being used by Him to affect and change our needy world.

Let's fill our lives, our homes and our churches with much prayer. Why settle for little, when we can have much? Let's not settle for the minimum, let's pray together, pray individually, and fill our homes with worship and prayer. May God bless you richly as you determine to create room in your home for prayer.

"The greatest warfare always surrounds your prayer life.
Nothing threatens hell more than a praying saint."

(Bob Sorge)

CHAPTER 8

What Jesus Taught About the Secret Place (2)

Praying the Lord's Prayer ...

Jesus not only told us *where* to pray (in the secret place), but He also taught us *what* to pray when we go there.

In Matthew 6:9, with the context still focused on prayer in the secret place, Jesus tells us how *not* to pray, and then He says:

"This, then, is how you should pray." (NIV)

The NKJV translates this verse,

"In this manner, therefore, pray."

What we call "the Lord's prayer" then, is not only a prayer that we can pray – with it Jesus provided us with a format for effective and holistic prayer in the secret place.

Jesus teaches us that such holistic prayer, behind closed doors, where we encounter the Father, should include the following elements:

1. Worship and adoration: *"Our Father in heaven, hallowed be Your Name."*

2. Prayer aligned with God's will: *"Your kingdom come, your will be done on earth as it is in heaven."* In other words, before we pray "My, my, my" we need to pray "Thy, Thy, Thy"! Before we begin to express to the Father what we want, we should pray for what *He wants* (I will elaborate on this thought later).

3. Daily prayer: *"Give us this day our daily bread."* Everything in
the Lord's prayer is to be prayed *daily*. Jesus invites us to
petition God for our needs and every day He wants to infuse
us with His grace, goodness and generosity.

4. Prayer for forgiveness: *"Forgive us our trespasses, as we forgive
those who trespass against us."* Everyday forgiveness is transacted
in two ways: towards and from God, and towards man.

5. Spiritual warfare: *"And do not lead us into temptation, but
deliver us from the evil one."* We are to be aware of spiritual
warfare and pray "deliver us from evil" every day. More on
this later.

6. Worship and adoration: *"For Yours is the kingdom and the
power and the glory for ever. Amen."* We close as we started,
worshipping and proclaiming God's greatness over our lives
and over everything we have prayed for.

In my teaching on the secret place I have often posed two
questions:

Q1: Why do so few Christians spend quality time alone with God each day?

I believe that the answer has to do with spiritual warfare. In
his excellent book, *Unrelenting Prayer*, Bob Sorge writes,

> The greatest warfare always surrounds your prayer life.
> Nothing threatens hell more than a praying saint. When
> you're abiding in His presence, clinging to His love, living
> in His word, holding to His promise, remaining fervent
> in spirit, and believing for His visitation, you are an
> explosion that's waiting to happen. Don't think your enemy
> will let you inhabit God's promises unchallenged ... The
> battle to pray and keep on praying has never been fiercer.

Q2: Why is it that some Christians dont develop properly in spirit and character, even though they pray a lot?

Unfortunately, I have to admit that I have met some Christians who pray frequently but are still weak in character and in the fruit of the Holy Spirit. I have travelled in and out of many nations and the fruit of the Spirit as listed in Galatians 5:22-23 looks the same everywhere:

"But the fruit of the Spirit is love, joy, peace, longsuffering, kindness, goodness, faithfulness, gentleness, self-control."

How can some people who pray and intercede a great deal, still be proud, abrasive, rude, unforgiving and lacking in grace? It seems like a contradiction and could even put some people off praying.

I believe that one of the reasons for this is that they do not pray in the way that Jesus taught us to pray in Matthew 6:9-15. According to Jesus' format, worship, selflessness, repentance, forgiveness and heart searching are high on the agenda. We not only need to be in the secret place daily, but we need to pray as Jesus taught us, covering all the bases of holistic prayer. Then, of course, we must live a life of faith, trust and obedience.

"Our father, who art in heaven, hallowed be your name."

(Matthew 6:9)

"Devotion belongs to the inner life and lives in the closet,
but also appears in the public services of the sanctuary.
It is part of the very spirit of true worship and is
of the nature of the spirit of prayer."

(E. M. Bounds, *The Essentials of Prayer*)

CHAPTER 9

What Jesus Taught
About the Secret Place
(3)

Patterns for prayer ...

The Lord teaches us that our first focus for prayer in the secret place, should be "our Father in heaven."

1. *"Our Father in heaven, hallowed be Your Name"* (Matthew 6:9) is *worship*. We begin our time in the secret place with worship, taking our eyes off the earth and focusing on Heaven. Here we bypass our circumstances, problems, needs and satanic assaults, to focus on Him – the Most High, the Almighty – our Father in Heaven. We lift up His name in worship and in praise and adoration, and His greatness is superimposed over all the situations of our life.

   Worship and praise is a vital part of prayer in the secret place. Let's simply highlight a few things concerning worship:

   Worship takes our minds off ourselves and focuses on God.
   Worship helps to align our lives with God.
   Worship brings the atmosphere of Heaven down to Earth.
   Worship and praise can bind and scatter the enemy as we read in Psalm 149 and 2 Chronicles 20 with King Jehoshaphat.

   So begin your time in the secret place by lifting up the Father's name in worship and praise. Be creative and varied each day.

2. *"Your kingdom come, Your will be done on earth, as it is in heaven"* (Matthew 6:10). As we assert God's kingship and authority we are submitting afresh to His rule and reign.

Every day I pray for His kingdom to come and His will to be done in:

my life
my family
our church
our town/city and nation

There are so many ways to approach these prayers creatively. Be led and inspired by the Holy Spirit. He is there to help us.

I taught on the sections that follow in my first book, *Answered Prayer is God's Will For You.* Let these headings serve as guidelines as you cover important areas each day in prayer and intercession.

3. *"Give us this day our **daily** bread"* (Matthew 6:11). As we read the whole of the Lord's prayer in context, we clearly see that the secret place is a daily appointment/encounter. Jesus invites us every day, i.e. "this day", to ask Him for the things we need. Jesus is the *"bread of life"*:

> *"And Jesus said to them, 'I am the bread of life. He who comes to Me shall never hunger, and he who believes in Me shall never thirst.'"* (John 6:35)

> *"The Jews then complained about Him, because He said, 'I am the bread which came down from heaven.'"* (John 6:41)

> *"I am the bread of life."* (John 6:48)

Every day we can put our urgent requests before the Father in prayer:

> *"Ask, and it will be given to you; seek, and you will find; knock, and it will be opened to you. For everyone who asks receives, and he who seeks finds, and to him who knocks it will be opened."* (Matthew 7:7-8)

We belong to a prayer-answering God. As we spend time on each section, we can be assured that we are praying according to the teachings of the Lord as recorded in Scripture.

I do not always spend the same amount of time on each section. Sometimes it may be a few seconds, sometimes several minutes, but I always cover each section in prayer each day.

I also take the time to read the Word, pray in tongues and pray over important issues each day.

4. *"And forgive us our debts* [sins, trespasses] *as we forgive our debtors* [those who have sinned against us]." (Matthew 6:12). Daily self-examination is vital for keeping our lives pure and holy. Jesus teaches us to receive and release forgiveness every day as we fellowship with Him in the secret place.

I love to pray Psalm 19:14 regularly:

> *"Let the words of my mouth and the meditation of my heart*
> *be acceptable in Your sight,*
> *O LORD, my strength and my Redeemer."*

Another prayer I pray in my ongoing quest to live a holy life is inspired by another passage in the Sermon on the Mount (Matthew 6:22-23), where Jesus describes how people should live under God's reign:

> *"The lamp of the body is the eye. If therefore your eye is good, your whole body will be full of light."* (v22)

Wow! Doesn't that sound good? I pray the following and you can pray it too:

> "Lord, let my eye be good, so that my whole body will be full of light."

It is so good to have a thorough clean out every day, making sure we have not allowed darkness to accumulate in our lives, because we read that conversely,

"... If your eye is bad, your whole body will be full of darkness. If therefore the light that is in you is darkness, how great is that darkness!" (v23)

Let us pray like David the psalmist (Psalm 51:10):

"Create in me a clean heart, O God,
and renew a steadfast spirit within me."

5. *"And do not lead us into temptation, but deliver us from the evil one"* (Matthew 6:13). Jesus told His disciples in Gethsemane, as He tells us today:

"Watch and pray, lest you enter into temptation. The spirit indeed is willing, but the flesh is weak." (Matthew 26:41)

Each day in the secret place we are being prepared for another day of walking with God. As part of our preparation for the day we pray that we will not be caught or ensnared by temptation and we ask God to deliver us from evil. It is biblical to pray for deliverance from evil.

Remember that this section comes towards the end of our prayer programme, and is not meant to be the only focus, but *one* of our priorities in prayer.

I use this time to do spiritual warfare. I declare that the devil is bound off my life, family, church and ministry. I believe God for His protection and provision for the day.

As our prayer life and intimacy grows, we find the Lord teaching us new ways to be creative and effective in prayer.

Jesus said in Matthew 26:40:

"What! Could you not watch with Me one hour?"

I teach and encourage people to spend an hour with the Lord each day. During this hour we should read God's Word (systematically if possible), use the Lord's prayer format, and pray in tongues if you have that wonderful gift. Paul said (1 Corinthians 14:14a):

> *"For if I pray in a tongue, my spirit prays."*

Tongues doesn't make us better than anyone else, it just makes us "better", giving us a wider scope in prayer.

I encourage people to aim for an hour in the secret place, but if you cannot manage an hour, go for half an hour, or break it up into 15-minute sections throughout the day.

We must understand that God loves us whether we spend time in prayer or not. But in prayer *we are the ones who benefit.* There is so much that God wants to pour into our lives each day, but remember, when we miss a day, God is not disappointed *with us* – He is disappointed *for us.* He loves us to come into His presence day after day. The cumulative effect will be seen by all and will release from God an "open reward" (Matthew 6:6):

> *"Pray to your Father who is in the secret place; and your Father who sees in secret will reward you openly."*

6. Finally: *"For Yours is the kingdom and the power and the glory forever. Amen"* (Matthew 6:13b). As we begin to finish our private time alone with Him in the secret place, once again, following His teaching and instructions, we worship, praise and thank Him for His kingdom, power and glory.

After this we can enter our day ready for anything and everything. We come out of our secret place confident that God is with us and for us, and that He will lead us to navigate and negotiate another fruitful day.

"Every moment you spend in the secret place is an investment. You are investing into eternal realities. God makes note of your labours and considers how he will honour your devotion. And seeds are being planted in your heart that will bring forth a harvest in your own heart – if you continue to persevere in faith and love . . . so don't quit . . . Catch the secret: he who sows will most assuredly reap."

(Bob Sorge)

CHAPTER 10

The Rewards of the Secret Place

(1)

*"He who **dwells** in the secret place
of the Most High ..."*
(Psalm 91:1a)

It is the person who dwells in this secret place who *"shall abide
under the shadow of the Almighty"*. As we fellowship with Him
day after day, alone behind a closed door, meeting the Father,
imperceptibly something begins to happen. We abide under His
shadow. That is intimacy.

In his awesome book, *The Secrets of the Secret Place*, Bob
Sorge says:

> When we step into the presence of God we are exposing
> ourselves to externally powerful forces. Everything
> within us changes when we touch the radiating glory
> that emits from His face. *'For the Lord God is a sun'*
> (Psalm 84:11). The Sun provides heat, light, energy and
> ultraviolet rays – radiation when we place ourselves in
> the sun of His Countenance – the radiation of His glory
> does violence to those cancerous iniquities that we often
> feel helpless to overcome. Time in His presence is perhaps
> the most potent procedure to deal with the chronic sin
> issues that plague us.

Just as Moses' face was shining when he came down from the
mountain of God's presence, we too will begin to shine as we
meet with the Father in the secret place. Bob Sorge calls it

"radiation therapy" as God begins to infuse us with new passions and desires that come from Him. Psalm 16:11 says:

> *"You will show me the path of life;*
> *in Your presence is fullness of joy;*
> *at Your right hand are pleasures forevermore."*

I believe that Psalm 91 is a list of rewards that come to the person who dwells in the secret place. I believe that God showed me that *everything* in Psalm 91 is reserved by God especially for secret place dwellers. All these supernatural blessings, answers to prayer, protection and miraculous interventions are not automatic in the life of every believer, but flow from those who *"dwell in the secret place of the Most High."*

I believe that many of the "open rewards" that Jesus referred to in Matthew 6 are listed here in Psalm 91. There may be more, but it is a wonderful and comprehensive list. So let us uncover the promises God has made to the *secret place dweller.*

"To strive in prayer means to struggle through those hindrances which would prevent us entirely from continuing in persevering prayer. It means to be so watchful at all times that we notice when we become slothful in prayer, and that we can go to the spirit of prayer to have this remedied."

(Dr O. Hallesby)

CHAPTER 11

The Rewards of the Secret Place

(2)

Confidence in God ...

One of my greatest joys as a minister is to see how people begin to mature rapidly when they begin to spend quality and quantity time with the Lord.

I have often said that "one of the greatest problems Christians face is that they do not know God very well." We only get to know people as we spend time with them. It is the same with our God. That is one of the main reasons why the secret place is so special. It breeds intimacy with God.

"He who dwells in the secret place of the Most High shall abide under the shadow of the Almighty" (Psalm 91:1)

This is one of the first benefits listed in the psalm. We will experience a great closeness with the Lord.

In verse 2 it says:

"I will say of the Lord, 'He is my refuge and my fortress; my God, in Him I will trust.'"

As we dwell in that secret place, living our lives out of it, a holy confidence in Him begins to grow in us and we hear ourselves saying, *"He is my refuge and my fortress."* Imagine God being a fortress around you.

"Refuge" means "a shelter or protection from danger or trouble". "Fortress" means "a fortified place, a defence".

The dweller of the secret place develops a confidence in the God he is getting to know and so he declares boldly, "This God whose shadow I am under is my shelter from danger and trouble. He is my defence and my fortress, and I will trust Him at all times."

As we live out of the secret place we understand that we can experience supernatural deliverance again and again.

> *"Yes, we had the sentence of death in ourselves, that we should not trust in ourselves but in God who raises the dead, who delivered us from so great a death, and does deliver us; in whom we trust that He will still deliver us, you also help-ing together in prayer for us, that thanks may be given by many persons on our behalf for the gift granted to us through many."* (2 Corinthians 1:9-11).

> *"Surely He shall deliver you from the snare of the fowler and from the perilous pestilence."* (Psalm 91:3)

A fowler is someone who catches birds in a trap or snare. The Lord promises us that, under His shadow, there is deliverance from various snares and traps and strategies of the enemy. There is also supernatural deliverance from all kinds of pestilence because,

> *"He shall cover you with His feathers, and under His wings you shall take refuge."* (v4a)

One of the open rewards of the secret place is that many things that affect others around you won't touch you.

As we fellowship with Him and live our lives serving Him and people, as He has instructed us,

> *"His truth shall be your shield and buckler."* (v4b)

Another version translates this, *"His faithful promises are your armour and protection."*

Am I saying that we will never have any trials and tribulations? No. We will see later that He is with us in trouble.

As this person dwells in the secret place there is much supernatural protection for them. We are talking about someone who has made a determined decision to be with the Lord daily.

This does not mean we work to earn our salvation, because we are already saved. There is no clash here with the grace message, because the Bible teaches us that we access grace when we boldly come into His presence (Hebrews 4:16):

> *"Let us therefore come boldly to the throne of grace, that we may obtain mercy and find grace to help in time of need."*

I don't know about you, but my "time of need" is every day, and I come boldly before His throne for grace to be released in full measure every day

Further benefits and rewards for the secret place dweller:

> *"You shall not be afraid of the terror by night,*
> *nor of the arrow that flies by day ..."* (v5)

> *"... nor of the pestilence that walks in darkness,*
> *nor of the destruction that lays waste at noonday..."* (v6)

> *"A thousand may fall at your side,*
> *and ten thousand at your right hand;*
> *but it shall not come near you."* (v7)

Does that sound like supernatural protection? I think it does.

Can you imagine someone like David hearing this when he was being pursued by Saul? Certainly David and his mighty men lived in this kind of dimension.

The promises and open rewards for those who dwell in the secret place go on:

> *"Only with your eyes shall you look,*
> *and see the reward of the wicked."* (v8)

And just look at the following verses:

> *"Because you have made the Lord, who is my refuge,*
>   *even the Most High, your dwelling place,*
> *no evil shall befall you,*
>   *nor shall any plague come near your dwelling."* (v9-10)

> *"For He shall give His angels charge over you,*
>   *to keep you in all your ways."* (v11)

> *"In their hands they shall bear you up,*
>   *lest you dash your foot against a stone."* (v12)

This passage goes on to say that the dweller in the secret place has a special hedge around his or her life because of devotion to the Most High God. God delights to put a hedge of supernatural protection around His people. He put a hedge around Job and, when it came down, Job suffered a great deal. But after a period of trials and tribulations, God restored the hedge around Job's life and blessed Him for years to come. Some have said that Job's difficulties lasted less than a year, but when the Most High restored his hedge of protection, Satan was held at bay, as God blessed Job abundantly (Job 42:12-17):

> *"Now the LORD blessed the latter days of Job more than his beginning; for he had fourteen thousand sheep, six thousand camels, one thousand yoke of oxen, and one thousand female donkeys. He also had seven sons and three daughters. And he called the name of the first Jemimah, the name of the second Keziah, and the name of the third Keren-Happuch. In all the land were found no women so beautiful as the daughters of Job; and their father gave them an inheritance among their brothers.*

> *After this Job lived one hundred and forty years, and saw his children and grandchildren for four generations. So Job died, old and full of days."*

We will continue to explore Psalm 91 in the next chapter.

"No one is a firmer believer in the
power of prayer than the devil;
not that he practices it, but he suffers from it."

(Guy H. King)

CHAPTER 12

The Rewards of the Secret Place

(3)

Promises of Psalm 91...

I was so excited about being in Kansas City in the USA. I remembered the songs I sang as a boy: "I'm going to Kansas City... Kansas City, here I come." Wow! And here I was in Kansas City.

It was April 2007 and, following a prophecy I had received in London around 2001 from a well known prophet, I was there to check out the International House of Prayer (IHOP) where there was 24/7 prayer, praise and worship going up before the Lord, all day every day. The 2001 prophecy had said that our church in Wembley would one day house a 24/7 house of prayer. So I had travelled to Kansas to study the dynamics of how it worked.

I arrived from London in the evening and went to stay with a young Christian family for my eight-day visit. I had dinner with my hosts and thought I would retire early so as to go fresh to IHOP in the morning. I went to bed about 9pm, telling the Lord that I needed a good night's sleep before I stepped out into my exciting tomorrow.

I awoke abruptly after an hour or so, however, with pains in my lower abdomen. I immediately began to massage my stomach and pray. The pain continued to get worse and soon I found myself vomiting violently in the basin in the kitchen. I was staying in a little self-contained flat and was embarrassed, hoping my host could not hear what was happening.

I vomited on and off for a long time until my sides began to hurt. I continued to pray, but the pains only grew worse. I prayed in tongues, walked around, lay on the floor, knelt, rolled on the floor, and asked the Lord to heal me.

There was a storm in my brain: "Your trip is ruined, you need to send for an ambulance; it's going to cost you to receive medical attention in America." All the time I was praying and trying to phone home to ask for prayer, but I could not get through. I asked my hosts to pray for me and returned to my room.

After an hour or more of praying in tongues and crying out to the Lord, I began to say to Him, "Holy Spirit, You are my Comforter, my Helper and my Teacher. Please help me and counsel me, my Counsellor, and please tell me what is happening." To my surprise, I heard the Lord clearly say the word "Satanist". I was befuddled and bewildered. What could this possibly mean? I later found out from my hosts that there were satanic people living opposite and that they were often attacked at night by spirits.

Goodness me! I came for a rest, not a fight. I was completely unprepared and forgot to plead the Blood over my room and bind the enemy, as I always did whenever I travelled anywhere. I thought I was safe and forgot to dedicate my abode to the Lord, as it was my habit to do.

After nearly two hours of prayer, praying in tongues and crying out to the Lord, I said to Him, "Lord, you said 'Satanist' so I know I'm in warfare, but what do I do now, since the pain is still here? Please help me." I heard the Lord whisper another word to me: "Test". As I began to process what this meant, I continued to pray, encouraged by what I heard, and asked the Lord to heal, restore and speak to me again. I understood that my faith was being tested and I persisted in prayer, looking to the Lord for His mercy and healing.

After more than two hours of prayer, a holy determination rose up in me. I said to the Lord, "I have only one option now: health and healing. There will be no Option 2. I'm believing and trusting You and Your Word. No ambulance, no doctor, no phone calls, just me and You."

After around 2½ hours of praying in tongues and English and crying out to God, I clearly heard the Lord say, "Sword." As I processed this, I understood that now the Lord wanted me to use the Word as a sword to gain victory. As I quoted Scripture to God and at the devil, and as I spoke God's Word into my body, after nearly three hours of prayer I was completely healed: the pain left, the vomiting stopped, and I had a great enlightening time at IHOP for the next seven days.

That was quite a battle! But thanks be to God, who gives us the victory. To Him be all the glory.

Verse 13 of Psalm 91 reads,

> *"You shall tread upon the lion and the cobra,*
> *the young lion and the serpent you shall trample underfoot."*

This speaks of victory in spiritual warfare. Spiritual warfare is real and sometimes there are casualties. Sometimes battles are lost for many and varied reasons. Because we *"dwell in the secret place"* it does not mean we won't face any battles. But we take comfort from God's promise that,

> *"Because he has set his love upon Me, therefore I will deliver him;*
> *I will set him on high, because he has known My name."*
> (v14)

God says that He will reward openly those who dwell in the secret place, and He promises that that person will experience the wonderful promises of Psalm 91. Since I have practiced Psalm 91:1, I have found that the promises made by the Lord in this psalm *work*! I am prepared to live one day at a time for the rest of my life trusting that He will do what He says.

I believe that Paul was a Psalm 91 person. In spite of all his difficulties, trials and tribulations, he was able to fulfil his calling. To die as a martyr is a special privilege given by God and, if He ever calls us to martyrdom He will give us the grace for it. This eventually happened to Paul, but while he was still living out his destiny he was shielded under the wing of the Almighty. No one could kill him before his time.

Let's put our trust in what God says in His Word. I cannot live my life by what man experiences. I must live my life according to His promises. When we go through periods of suffering, He promises to be with us:

> *"He shall call upon Me, and I will answer him;*
> *I will be with him in trouble;*
> *I will deliver him and honour him."* (Psalm 91:15)

I have found this scripture to be true. In Kansas City, when I called Him, He answered me. He was with me in my trouble and He delivered me.

I have had my fair share of difficulties, trials and tribulations over the years. Life is not always easy. Difficult people, difficult circumstances, trials, tribulations and satanic assaults come and go.

But many Christians live in defeat, in bondage to sin, self and Satan, when they do not need to. Most Christians do not dwell in the secret place of the Most High. I estimate that more than 95% of Christians in the western world don't know what it is like to live intimately with Christ and dwell consistently in God's presence. As a result, many fall and go under with sin, sickness, compromise and defeat.

God has an answer. We may not be able to answer every difficult question, but let's not throw away Scripture because we know people who have not experienced victory (more about this later).

Jesus said, *"Go into your room and shut the door . . ."* (Matthew 6:6) and promised that we would meet with the Father there and that He would reward us openly. Psalm 91 invites us to experience the benefits and rewards of the secret place. It is a message given by the Lord to call His body, His Bride, into a place of intimacy with Him.

Dwelling in the secret place requires a "violent" or determined decision to go to bed on time, wake up and prioritise our time with Him. The distractions are many, but oh, it is worth it! Come into that place of intimacy and trust with Him, and allow Him to invade your life with His miraculous interventions.

"The prayer closet is not an asylum for the indolent and worthless Christian. It is not a nursery where none but babes belong. It is a battlefield of the Church, its citadel, the scene of heroic unearthly conflicts."

(E. M. Bounds)

CHAPTER 13

Some Important Considerations

Prayer beyond ourselves ...

In this book I have not tried to address every aspect of the Christian life or the various problems, difficulties, trials and tribulations that Christians face worldwide. In this chapter, therefore, I want to take some time to look at a few of the wider issues and their relation to prayer.

Praying for nations

Scripture is clear in declaring that God can change the atmosphere in a whole nation, if that nation will only respond to His call, His counsel and His wisdom.

God can change not only our lives, but He can change marriages, homes, families, churches, towns, villages and, yes, whole nations. The Bible and history record many instances where our Lord God intervened and delivered even a whole nation in answer to the prayers of God's people.

Let's examine the following scripture (1 Timothy 2:1-4). In it we see a clear call to pray for those in authority in our nation and an explanation of why this is so important:

> *"Therefore I exhort first of all that supplications, prayers, intercessions, and giving of thanks be made for all men ..."*
> *"... for kings and all who are in authority, that we may lead a quiet and peaceable life in all godliness and reverence."*

> *"For this is good and acceptable in the sight of God our Saviour..."*
>
> *"...who desires all men to be saved and to come to the knowledge of the truth."*

We are clearly exhorted in the scripture above to pray for our governments, for politicians and people of influence in our lands. I must admit that for many years I had a very casual attitude towards this scripture – and I was not alone, for many Christians and denominations have severely neglected the counsel of Paul and the Lord in this scripture, some making only token gestures and sending up only minimal prayer for the nation where they live. This has gone on for years, decades and centuries in many nations of the world.

I have read accounts where the Christians in a nation were warned prophetically of disasters and persecutions to come, but still neglected serious prayer for their nation, until eventually the whole nation was plunged into darkness. The way back from such a situation is long and hard.

But if we, as God's people in our nation, seriously pray for our land, God will do what He promises He will do: He will influence and appoint good governments, and bless our lands with peace, so that the Gospel can flourish in them.

Serious prayer in any nation can result in God's influence being released in great measure to bring change, outpourings and even major revivals.

In his inspiring book, *Prayer Generals*, Theo Effiong writes:

At the turn of the century revival fires began burning in certain places of the world. The Welsh revival that came in late 1904 under Evan Roberts was one of them. The Sialkot revival in Punjab, India under Praying Hyde, that burst out in 1905 to 1906 was another. Indeed, the ten years from 1901 to 1910 were termed the "Revival Decade". Other nations that reported revival fires within this decade were Australia, New Zealand, Japan, Indonesia, Scandinavia, Korea and China, to mention a few. Los Angeles, California, was another place where revival fires were brewing. The entire city was already on the verge of a great spiritual happening. In the midst of this there was one man in particular that availed himself unto the Lord, making revival a reality. That man was William Seymour.'

All these revivals were triggered and spread through much prayer, often initially emitting from the prayers of a single person.

God promises to heal a nation

In the second book of Chronicles we have a promise given to Solomon as he is dedicating the temple on its completion:

"When Solomon had finished praying, fire came down from heaven and consumed the burnt offering and the sacrifices; and the glory of the LORD filled the temple." (2 Chronicles 7:1)

We read of tongues of fire coming down on each one when 120 people prayed for ten days and revival broke out and began to spread across the globe:

"When the Day of Pentecost had fully come, they were all with one accord in one place. And suddenly there came a sound from heaven, as of a rushing mighty wind, and it filled the whole house where they were sitting. Then there appeared to them divided tongues, as of fire, and one sat upon each of them. And they were all filled with the Holy Spirit and began to speak with other tongues, as the Spirit gave them utterance." (Acts 2:1-4)

However, in 2 Chronicles 7:14 we have a unique promise given to Solomon and Israel, which the Holy Spirit has given to Christians in nations all over the globe, especially in recent times. This scripture promises that if God's people seek Him in serious prayer (and, I believe, with fasting and repentance since the word "humbling" or "humble" is often associated with fasting), God promises to hear, forgive and heal the nation:

> *"If My people who are called by My name will humble themselves, and pray and seek My face, and turn from their wicked ways, then I will hear from heaven, and will forgive their sin and heal their land."*

God promises to respond to the prayers and repentance of His people, so much so that a whole backslidden nation could be healed and set right by God.

There are so many nations in dire need of the interventions of God.

In the last few years I have felt very burdened for our nation, Great Britain. I have found myself recently praying for our Prime Minister, our politicians, the Royal Family and the Church daily. In our church we pray for our nation and for each of these people in authority every week, often several times a week, during various times of prayer.

Praying for Christians suffering persecution

There are many anti-Christian nations like China, Burma, North Korea and others, where there has been and is serious persecution of the saints. We who live in comparative freedom are exhorted in Scripture to pray for them as if we were with them in prison:

"Remember the prisoners as if chained with them – those who are mistreated – since you yourselves are in the body also." (Hebrews 13:3)

God is able to give us His heart for prayer and action out of the intimacy of the secret place. I was incredibly blessed to read *The Heavenly Man*, an account of a Chinese Christian minister, Brother Yun. This book combines a wonderful biography of Brother Yun with an account of the miraculous growth of the Chinese underground Church.

This book, like no other I have read (I have read it ten times to date), gives an account of a miracle working God answering prayers even in the midst of impossible situations. It has been a great inspiration to many, showing that God responds to prayer wherever people pray and trust Him. Each time I have read it I have rejoiced, wept, laughed and been inspired. It could be that China now has more born again Christians than any other nation on earth.

The secret place then is not only a place of personal prayer. It automatically becomes, under His inspiration, a place from which we grow to pray way beyond the borders of our personal needs.

The secret place is *God's best for us.* It is the foundation from which we live our lives. God invites us into the secret place regardless of where we live and how we live, and regardless of our circumstances, pressures, comforts or situations. If for some reason we are unable to find a secret place God will give His grace and compensate for us.

Brother Yun fasted and prayed for 75 days under the most adverse conditions. In fact, his prayers could have been a catalyst for prayer and revival to be multiplied across China. He writes:

More than 70 days had passed and I hadn't eaten any food or drunk any water in all that time ... At that time

I felt that an angel of the Lord surrounded me and kept me from dying ... On the 75th day of my fast, around 3.00am, a brilliant light flooded my cell.

After being bullied, tortured, urinated on, electrocuted and grossly mistreated, he writes:

During the long fast my days were full of struggle, miracles, dreams, visions and revelation from the Lord. I experienced His strength every day. Although I had no Bible, I meditated on His Word constantly from the scriptures I had memorised.

The secret place is a call from Heaven to God's people everywhere. The Lord wants to invade our lives with His goodness and grace wherever we are.

In conclusion, let's examine the following passage from the book of Acts and witness the effects of prayer:

"Now about that time Herod the king stretched out his hand to harass some from the church. Then he killed James the brother of John with the sword. And because he saw that it pleased the Jews, he proceeded further to seize Peter also. Now it was during the Days of Unleavened Bread. So when he had arrested him, he put him in prison, and delivered him to four squads of soldiers to keep him, intending to bring him before the people after Passover.

Peter was therefore kept in prison, but constant prayer was offered to God for him by the church. And when Herod was about to bring him out, that night Peter was sleeping, bound with two chains between two soldiers; and the guards before the door were keeping the prison. Now behold, an angel of the Lord stood by him, and a light shone in the prison; and he struck Peter on the side and raised him up, saying, 'Arise quickly!' And his chains fell off his hands.

Then the angel said to him, 'Gird yourself and tie on your sandals'; and so he did. And he said to him, 'Put on your garment and follow me.' So he went out and followed him, and did not know that what was done by the angel was real, but thought he was seeing a vision. When they were past the first and the second guard posts, they came to the iron gate that leads to the city, which opened to them of its own accord; and they went out and went down one street, and immediately the angel departed from him.

And when Peter had come to himself, he said, 'Now I know for certain that the Lord has sent His angel, and has delivered me from the hand of Herod and from all the expectation of the Jewish people.'

So, when he had considered this, he came to the house of Mary, the mother of John whose surname was Mark, where many were gathered together praying. And as Peter knocked at the door of the gate, a girl named Rhoda came to answer. When she recognized Peter's voice, because of her gladness she did not open the gate, but ran in and announced that Peter stood before the gate. But they said to her, 'You are beside yourself!' Yet she kept insisting that it was so. So they said, 'It is his angel.'

Now Peter continued knocking; and when they opened the door and saw him, they were astonished. But motioning to them with his hand to keep silent, he declared to them how the Lord had brought him out of the prison. And he said, 'Go, tell these things to James and to the brethren.' And he departed and went to another place.

Then, as soon as it was day, there was no small stir among the soldiers about what had become of Peter. But when Herod had searched for him and not found him, he examined the guards and commanded that they should be put to death.

And he went down from Judea to Caesarea, and stayed there." (Acts 12:1-19)

In verses 1-2, James the beloved apostle is killed by Herod. This was a great loss to the Church, he was one of the three who often accompanied Jesus. Then Herod seizes Peter, puts him in prison and probably wanted to execute him as well. But look at verse 5:

*"Peter was therefore kept in prison, **but constant prayer was offered to God for him by the church.**"*

As the church begins to pray, crying out to God, Peter is miraculously delivered. Note also verse 12 that mentions, *"many were gathered together praying"*.

Look also at the apostle Paul's experiences of being helped in prayer:

"Blessed be the God and Father of our Lord Jesus Christ, the Father of mercies and God of all comfort, who comforts us in all our tribulation, that we may be able to comfort those who are in any trouble, with the comfort with which we ourselves are comforted by God. For as the sufferings of Christ abound in us, so our consolation also abounds through Christ. Now if we are afflicted, it is for your consolation and salvation, which is effective for enduring the same sufferings which we also suffer. Or if we are comforted, it is for your consolation and salvation. And our hope for you is steadfast, because we know that as you are partakers of the sufferings, so also you will partake of the consolation.

For we do not want you to be ignorant, brethren, of our trouble which came to us in Asia: that we were burdened beyond measure, above strength, so that we despaired even of life. Yes, we had the sentence of death in ourselves, that we should not trust in ourselves but in God who raises the dead, who delivered us from so great a death, and does deliver us; in whom we trust that He will still deliver us, you also helping together in prayer for us, that thanks may be given by many persons on our behalf for the gift granted to us through many." (2 Corinthians 1:3-11)

In these verses Paul shares about a seriously stressful time which he experienced in Asia. Look especially at the last three verses:

"Yes, we had the sentence of death in ourselves, that we should not trust in ourselves but in God who raises the dead . . ." (v9)

". . . who delivered us from so great a death, and does deliver us; in whom we trust that He will still deliver us . . ." (v10)

". . . you also helping together in prayer for us, that thanks may be given by many persons on our behalf for the gift granted to us through many." (v11)

Paul spoke of his difficulty and his deliverance. He also spoke about being helped in prayer. In Paul's call, Jesus stated that he would suffer much. Apostles seem to have a special grace to endure suffering. The Lord spoke to Ananias, saying in Acts 9:15-16:

"But the Lord said to him, 'Go, for he is a chosen vessel of Mine to bear My name before Gentiles, kings, and the children of Israel. For I will show him how many things he must suffer for My name's sake.'"

Paul was an amazing man of prayer. I once did a study of his life, recording the prayers he prayed, his prayer life and prayer experiences (visions etc), and his constant requests for others to pray for him. I also recorded his many teachings and exhortations to pray, for example Colossians 4:2-4:

> *"Continue earnestly in prayer, being vigilant in it with thanksgiving; meanwhile praying also for us, that God would open to us a door for the word, to speak the mystery of Christ, for which I am also in chains, that I may make it manifest, as I ought to speak."*

Corporate prayer and fasting

Finally, in the book of Joel, we see a nation in disarray. Joel prophesied at a time of great devastation to the entire land of Judah. At the time, Judah was a nation with every problem imaginable: famine, starvation, social and economic problems, drink problems, family problems etc.

Three times a trumpet call goes out calling the nation to fasting, prayer and repentance. God promises a full restoration of everything, similar to 2 Chronicles 7:14:

> *"If My people who are called by My name will humble themselves, and pray and seek My face, and turn from their wicked ways, then I will hear from heaven, and will forgive their sin and heal their land."*

It is in the context of corporate fasting and prayer and repentance that the Lord says:

> *"And it shall come to pass afterward*
> *That I will pour out My Spirit on all flesh;*
> *Your sons and your daughters shall prophesy,*
> *Your old men shall dream dreams,*
> *Your young men shall see visions.*
> *And also on My menservants and on My maidservants*

I will pour out My Spirit in those days.
And I will show wonders in the heavens and in the earth:
Blood and fire and pillars of smoke.
The sun shall be turned into darkness,
And the moon into blood,
Before the coming of the great and awesome day of the LORD.
And it shall come to pass
That whoever calls on the name of the LORD
Shall be saved.
For in Mount Zion and in Jerusalem there shall be deliverance,
As the LORD has said,
Among the remnant whom the LORD calls." (Joel 2:28-32)

Dr Derek Prince points out in his modern day classic *Shaping History Through Prayer and Fasting*, that God will pour out His Spirit anywhere and everywhere where people corporately begin to fast and pray and call out to Him.

Yes, the Lord can begin to lay His burdens for prayer upon us, but it all begins to percolate out of the secret place.

As I said earlier, there is private, personal prayer, family prayer, church corporate prayer, inter-church prayer, denominational prayer, national prayer and worldwide prayer. *God wants to call a praying people into higher and deeper levels of prayer, intercession and warfare.*

"Then He came to His disciples and found them sleeping, and said to Peter, 'What? Could you not watch with Me one hour? Watch and pray, lest you enter into temptation. The spirit indeed is willing, but the flesh is weak.'"

(Matthew 26:40-41)

CHAPTER 14

Practical Help for Implementing the Secret Place

Finding your secret place …

The results of Psalm 91 are the release of the miraculous. Let's read these verses once more:

> *"He who dwells in the secret place of the Most High*
> *shall abide under the shadow of the Almighty.*
> *I will say of the Lord, 'He is my refuge and my fortress;*
> *my God, in Him I will trust.'*
> *Surely He shall deliver you from the snare of the fowler*
> *and from the perilous pestilence.*
> *He shall cover you with His feathers,*
> *and under His wings you shall take refuge;*
> *His truth shall be your shield and buckler.*
> *You shall not be afraid of the terror by night,*
> *nor of the arrow that flies by day,*
> *nor of the pestilence that walks in darkness,*
> *nor of the destruction that lays waste at noonday.*
> *A thousand may fall at your side,*
> *and ten thousand at your right hand;*
> *but it shall not come near you.*
> *Only with your eyes shall you look,*
> *and see the reward of the wicked.*
> *Because you have made the Lord, who is my refuge,*
> *even the Most High, your dwelling place,*
> *no evil shall befall you,*
> *nor shall any plague come near your dwelling;*

for He shall give His angels charge over you,
  to keep you in all your ways.
In their hands they shall bear you up,
  lest you dash your foot against a stone.
You shall tread upon the lion and the cobra,
  the young lion and the serpent you shall trample underfoot.
'Because he has set his love upon Me, therefore I will deliver him;
  I will set him on high, because he has known My name.
He shall call upon Me, and I will answer him;
  I will be with him in trouble;
  I will deliver him and honour him.
With long life I will satisfy him,
  and show him My salvation.'"

Let's now look in practical terms at how we can access the secret place daily.

As I've encouraged the reader throughout this book, I advise setting aside an hour each day to be alone with the Lord. It takes longer than we expect to silence the "noise" that life produces. But if, for whatever reason, a continuous hour is unmanageable, then begin with half an hour or break your prayer times into 15-minute sessions spread throughout the day.

During your time read the Word. I recommend reading the Bible right through in one year. A good place to start is with the gospels. Read one, two or three chapters a day. Read more if you can.

Above all, find a quiet room that is convenient for you and which you can make your personal "secret place" of intimacy with the Father.

When my daughter Angela was 12-years old, I taught her to pray for an hour a day. She prayed in her bedroom and used the following format:

20 minutes in tongues
20 minutes in English (using the Lord's prayer format)
20 minutes reading the Word

Personally, I like to pray in tongues a lot. I read the Bible, often the gospels, and follow a one-year Bible reading plan. Then I have a prayer list for myself, my family, the church etc, and I use the Lord's prayer format every day.

I used to prefer praying at night, but I asked the Lord to help me and I now pray in the mornings. But go with whatever works for you.

In addition to spending time with the Lord each day – for me it is more than an hour – occasionally I like to spend extended times with Him alone and in the Word and I teach others to do this.

I also like to go away periodically to spend one, two or three days alone in prayer, reading and studying the Word.

Establish your daily secret place alone with Him and develop your prayer life from there.

The secret place

As I have pondered the joys and benefits of the secret place I have put pen to paper to try and define all that it is and can be to the believer. The following expresses all that happens and can happen in our lives as we determine to dwell in that *secret place of the Most High*:

It's a time of intimacy
It's a time of cleansing
It's a time of healing
It's a time when forgiveness flows
It's a time of petitioning

It's a time of setting things in order
It's a time of revelation and reflection
It's a time of heart searching
It's a time of spiritual warfare
It's a time of releasing
It's a time of empowering

It's a time when we love Him, hear from Him, worship Him, believe Him, sacrifice to Him, submit to Him. It's a time when we receive strength and favour and revelation and direction, to live a focused and fruitful life for our Lord and Saviour.

It's a time of sowing and reaping.

The secret place is all the above and more.

"No man is greater than his prayer life …
Failing here, we fail everywhere."

(Leonard Ravenhill)

CHAPTER 15

Going Higher, Further and Deeper

Prayer and fasting…

There are many lessons to be learnt from Israel of old. At the burning bush, God identifies Himself to Moses as the God of Abraham, Isaac and Jacob:

> *"So when the LORD saw that he turned aside to look, God called to him from the midst of the bush and said, 'Moses, Moses!' And he said, 'Here I am.' Then He said, 'Do not draw near this place. Take your sandals off your feet, for the place where you stand is holy ground. I am the God of your ancestors,' he said, 'the God of Abraham, the God of Isaac and the God of Jacob.' At this Moses covered his face, for he was afraid to look at God."* (Exodus 3:4-6)

There is much we can learn from the lives of Abraham, Isaac and Jacob. We see God's way of dealing with His people from the way He deals with Abraham, Isaac and Jacob – an interesting study. God clearly wants the best for His people and we see how He blesses Abraham, Isaac and Jacob in spite of every trial, difficulty and mishap.

After the Lord changed Jacob's name to Israel and the nation began to grow and emerge with the formation of the twelve tribes, we see Israel being led out of captivity in Egypt by Moses and into the Promised Land by Joshua. The Law had been given under Moses and the people were given the precepts, principles and commands of God to live by.

However, after the death of Joshua right up to the appointment of King Saul, Israel was influenced and led by judges.

Israel continually did evil in the sight of the Lord and *"there was no king in Israel; everyone did what was right in his own eyes"* (Judges 21:25).

The people of Israel broke their covenant with the Lord by deliberately serving foreign gods. As a result the Lord delivered them into the hands of various oppressors. Each time the people cried out to the Lord, He raised up a judge to bring deliverance to them.

However, Israel's record and response to God, even under the kings of Israel and Judah, was very up and down. The usual sequence of events, apart from under the leadership of David and a few other godly kings like him, was abysmal: disobedience, judgement, crying out and restoration seemed to be an endless cycle that was repeated throughout the history of God's people.

Yet, we are told that these accounts were written *for our benefit* in order that we should learn from them.

I'm afraid that in recent history and in certain places and nations today, the Church has become compromised, cold and ineffectual. The Church itself has also experienced ups and downs and ins and outs not dissimilar to Israel. However, the good news is that *Jesus is building His Church* and He has brought us through the dark ages into times of reformation, revival, renewal and refreshing.

The Church is growing rapidly worldwide and is beginning to rise up to be the mighty force that we are meant to be. For the Bride of Christ to be ready for the return of the Bridegroom we are being prepared. Layer upon layer of truth has been restored to us, and more and more rapidly from the 1500s onwards.

So, from the foundation of intimacy and relationship the Lord would desire to take us up higher and deeper in Him. The

Israelites did not develop in relationship and passion for God and, as happens so often, if we are not moving forwards we start to move backwards. As we develop intimacy and passion for the Lord and capture His heart, He will lead us forward into more of His love and power and fruitfulness. Perhaps we will be the generation after God's own heart, like King David of old. A Psalm 91 person is drawn into being a person after God's own heart.

I look forward to my time with God each day in the secret place. It is not always easy and not always exciting. I don't always feel His presence in a tangible way but, every day as I spend time alone with Him He empowers and deposits what is needed for that day. I would put it this way: *I do not always feel elated or excited or full in the secret place but, if I ever miss it, I feel empty.* But remember that when you miss your time alone with God, He is not disappointed *with* you, just disappointed *for* you.

I cannot imagine trying to live out a day without the inner strength, grace and power that is released each day in and through the secret place.

Dr Paul Yonggi Cho has said:

> As pastor of the world's largest church, Satan is constantly trying to destroy me. So I cannot afford to miss one of my hours in prayer.

For him, I gather, it is four hours split up throughout the day.

As wonderful as time in the secret place is, there is more – yes, much more! The secret place is a necessary foundation from which we can launch out into deeper things.

Fasting an important key

Some of the greatest victories I have seen have come as a result of fasting and prayer. Jesus taught us that the Father has an "open reward" for those who fast in secret:

"Moreover, when you fast, do not be like the hypocrites, with a sad countenance. For they disfigure their faces that they may appear to men to be fasting. Assuredly, I say to you, they have their reward. But you, when you fast, anoint your head and wash your face, so that you do not appear to men to be fasting, but to your Father who is in the secret place; and your Father who sees in secret will reward you openly." (Matthew 6:16-18)

There are many good books available today that teach on prayer and fasting. There weren't many in the 60s and 70s. I have a whole chapter on fasting in my first book, *Answered Prayer is God's Will For You.* I do not intend to say a lot about the subject here (although one could easily write a whole book on it), but here are a few thoughts:

Two definitions:

Fasting is the practice of deliberately abstaining from food for spiritual purposes.

Fasting is the voluntary and deliberate abstinence from food for the purpose of concentrated prayer.

Suffice it to say that Moses fasted and so did Elijah, the prophets, Esther and others. We see the deliverance of an entire nation in the book of Esther as she calls God's people, through Mordecai, to fast:

"Then Esther told them to reply to Mordecai: 'Go, gather all the Jews who are present in Shushan, and fast for me; neither eat nor drink for three days, night or day. My maids and I will fast likewise. And so I will go to the king, which is against the law; and if I perish, I perish!'" (Esther 4:15-16)

In the New Testament we see Jesus beginning His ministry with a 40-day fast. We see John the Baptist and Anna the prophetess fasting before the Messiah is revealed. Fasting can be seen right throughout the Bible. *Fasting and prayer is a major key given to us by the Holy Spirit.*

Saul, who became Paul, fasted for three days and was healed and filled with the Holy Spirit at the end of his fast:

> *"And he was three days without sight, and neither ate nor drank. Now there was a certain disciple at Damascus named Ananias; and to him the Lord said in a vision, 'Ananias.' And he said, 'Here I am, Lord.'*
>
> *So the Lord said to him, 'Arise and go to the street called Straight, and inquire at the house of Judas for one called Saul of arsus, for behold, he is praying. And in a vision he has seen a man named Ananias coming in and putting his hand on him, so that he might receive his sight.'*
>
> *Then Ananias answered, 'Lord, I have heard from many about this man, how much harm he has done to Your saints in Jerusalem. And here he has authority from the chief priests to bind all who call on Your name.'*
>
> *But the Lord said to him, 'Go, for he is a chosen vessel of Mine to bear My name before Gentiles, kings, and the children of Israel. For I will show him how many things he must suffer for My name's sake.'*
>
> *And Ananias went his way and entered the house; and laying his hands on him he said, 'Brother Saul, the Lord Jesus, who appeared to you on the road as you came, has sent me that you may receive your sight and be filled with the Holy Spirit.' Immediately there fell from his eyes something like scales, and he received his sight at once; and he arose and was baptized.*

So when he had received food, he was strengthened. Then
Saul spent some days with the disciples at Damascus. "(Acts
9:9-19)

Fasting helps us to close down an area in our life (the longing
for food) so as to open up another side to become more sensitive
and open to Him. *Through fasting more of God's power and presence*
is released to help in situations of need.

Going aside to be alone with Him

In addition to spending time with Him alone in a secluded,
scheduled place behind a closed door in your room daily,
sometimes it is good to spend extended times with the Lord
in prayer and intercession, or simply seeking Him for guidance
and direction.

I often like to steal away for one, two or three days to read my
Bible, to pray and to just spend time tuning in to the Lord. As
a result I have often experienced meaningful times of increased
sensitivity and openness to Him whereby He has been able to
speak His will to me. Often I hear from the Lord after coming
back from being alone with Him.

Sometimes a crisis or a difficult situation may cause us to
spend extra time seeking Him and praying for breakthroughs
for our life, family, finances etc.

Here are a few suggestions:

You can block off a day's retreat to be alone in prayer and
the Word. Couples or church elders can schedule regular days
away for prayer. Sometimes ministers may choose to be away in
prayer and fasting for a week or more. Night prayer can be very
powerful, where we pray into the night for a season: once a week
from 12 midnight to 2.00am (or more); having a family week of

prayer – agreeing to pray at certain times of the day; husbands and wives scheduling a week of prayer (praying from say 12.00-2.00pm).

There are so many ways of increasing our times with Him. Some intercessors spend hours a day, scheduled and unscheduled, with Him.

We don't just pray for prayer's sake. Let's be specific in the things we pray for.

> *"Then He spoke a parable to them, that men always ought to pray and not lose heart, saying: 'There was in a certain city a judge who did not fear God nor regard man. Now there was a widow in that city; and she came to him, saying, "Get justice for me from my adversary." And he would not for a while; but afterward he said within himself, "Though I do not fear God nor regard man, yet because this widow troubles me I will avenge her, lest by her continual coming she weary me."'*
>
> *Then the Lord said, 'Hear what the unjust judge said. And shall God not avenge His own elect who cry out day and night to Him, though He bears long with them? I tell you that He will avenge them speedily. Nevertheless, when the Son of Man comes, will He really find faith on the earth?'"*
> (Luke 18:1-8).

*"And they were all filled with the Holy Spirit
and began to speak with other tongues,
as the Spirit gave them utterance."*

(Acts 2:4)

A Word About Prayer in Tongues

When I first encountered Christ and received Him as my Saviour and Lord, I was still a practising Catholic. I opened my heart to the Lord as a charismatic Catholic in late 1974. I was baptised in the Holy Spirit in St Hugh's Anglican Church in Luton, where Colin Urquhart was the minister, in April 1975.

I remember a group of people gathering around me to pray that I would receive the baptism of the Holy Spirit and the gift of tongues. As they prayed, I said to the Lord that I was not really sure that I wanted this gift. I was asking Him for other gifts at that time. Mind you, my Bible knowledge was so poor at the time that I was probably asking for gifts that did not exist. I do, however, remember saying, as I saw the enthusiasm of those around me, "Lord, if You want me to have this gift, I would like to receive it."

During that particular service, on a Sunday evening in April 1975, God touched my life in a remarkable way as I burst into tears, with my whole body vibrating as the power of the Holy Spirit came upon me. I had never, ever experienced anything like that before. This was a major turning point in my life.

After the service I asked to speak to Colin and, as I was waiting for him to finish ministering to someone else, I sat gingerly in the church casually glancing through my Bible. As I opened a page, the word "tongues" jumped out at me and, to my amazement, I began to speak in another tongue for the first time in my life.

I am so very grateful to the Lord for the gift of tongues and have grown to appreciate it more and more over the years and, indeed, I use it every day in prayer.

As Paul refers to tongues in 1 Corinthians 12 and 14 there is a difference between the *public gift*, which is *not for all*, and the *private gift*, which is *available to all* for edification and for prayer and worship.

I have had the privilege of praying for many over the years for the baptism of the Holy Spirit and they usually receive the gift of tongues within a few seconds.

In Acts 2, on the day of Pentecost, 120 people were filled with the Holy Spirit and spoke in tongues:

> *"And they were **all** filled with the Holy Spirit and began to speak with other tongues, as the Spirit gave them utterance."* (Acts 2:4)

We see the same thing happening in Acts 10 as the Holy Spirit falls on *"**many** Gentiles"* (Acts 10:27), and they begin to *"speak with tongues and magnify God"* (Acts 10:46).

And we see this happening once again in Acts 19:1-6:

> *"And it happened, while Apollos was at Corinth, that Paul, having passed through the upper regions, came to Ephesus. And finding some disciples he said to them, 'Did you receive the Holy Spirit when you believed?'*
>
> *So they said to him, 'We have not so much as heard whether there is a Holy Spirit.'*
>
> *And he said to them, 'Into what then were you baptized?'*
>
> *So they said, 'Into John's baptism.'*

Then Paul said, 'John indeed baptized with a baptism of repentance, saying to the people that they should believe on Him who would come after him, that is, on Christ Jesus.'

When they heard this, they were baptized in the name of the Lord Jesus. And when Paul had laid hands on them, the Holy Spirit came upon them, and they spoke with tongues and prophesied."

Paul says that, when we pray in tongues, we are praying with our spirit:

"For if I pray in a tongue, my spirit prays, but my under-standing is unfruitful. What is the conclusion then? I will pray with the spirit, and I will also pray with the understanding. I will sing with the spirit, and I will also sing with the understanding." (1 Corinthians 14:14-15)

I believe that tongues is a gift given to assist us in prayer. We receive an enlargement and an increased dimension of prayer as we pray in tongues.

In 1 Corinthians 14:18 Paul says:

"I thank my God I speak with tongues more than you all."

Some say, "Well, that great minister did not speak in tongues." I believe that tongues is available to all and is clear evidence of the initial filling of the Holy Spirit. We need to be filled with the Holy Spirit over and over again but, when we are "baptised in the Holy Spirit" we receive this wonderful gift to be used in prayer and intercession.

Speaking in tongues doesn't make us *better* than anyone else, it just makes us better, and, however great or small we may be, the gift of tongues enlarges us to be more effective in prayer and intercession.

If you have not received this wonderful gift, ask God to fill you today to overflowing with the Holy Spirit and to give you the gift of tongues.

It is reported that Katherine Kuhlman often prayed for long hours in tongues. Tongues can be a trigger for the supernatural gifts of the Holy Spirit. Ask Jesus for this gift and use it every day in your prayer time.

"God expounds more truths of prayer only to praying people ... Yes, unless you start praying, you can never learn the secrets of prayer."

(Ezekiel Francis)

APPENDIX 2

Avoiding Barriers and Blockages in Prayer

As we seek to get to know God better in our times of prayer in the secret place, let's make sure we don't allow anything to block or hinder us from continuing to grow close to the Lord.

We need to guard our relationship with God and with people. Jesus has commanded us to walk in love:

> *"A new commandment I give to you, that you love one another; as I have loved you, that you also love one another. By this all will know that you are My disciples, if you have love for one another."* (John 13:34-35)

Let's keep relationships right, forgiving quickly as the Lord forgives us. Mark 11:25-26 says in the context of prayer:

> *"And whenever you stand praying, if you have anything against anyone, forgive him, that your Father in heaven may also forgive you your trespasses. But if you do not forgive, neither will your Father in heaven forgive your trespasses."*

Let's keep our consciences clean, so that we can have confidence and faith.

> *"If someone says, 'I love God,' and hates his brother, he is a liar; for he who does not love his brother whom he has seen,*

how can he love God whom he has not seen? And this commandment we have from Him: that he who loves God must love his brother also." (1 John 4:20-21)

Let's not get involved in anything shady or dishonest. Let's guard what we watch with our eyes and listen to with our ears.

Remember: you always become like the people you mix with.

And whatever you give your attention to shapes your desires.

If we wish to dwell in the secret place God is calling us to a life of holiness. We may not be able to watch certain movies or programmes that others watch. Instead we remain open to God's guidance by His Holy Spirit:

> *"You will show me the path of life;*
> *in Your presence is fullness of joy;*
> *at Your right hand are pleasures for evermore."*
> (Psalm 16:11)

He has pleasures for us. His pleasures will satisfy us, so that we do not need the pleasures of sin and compromise.

Psalm 91

> *"He who dwells in the secret place of the Most High*
> *shall abide under the shadow of the Almighty.*
> *I will say of the Lord, 'He is my refuge and my fortress;*
> *my God, in Him I will trust.'*
> *Surely He shall deliver you from the snare of the fowler*
> *and from the perilous pestilence.*
> *He shall cover you with His feathers,*
> *and under His wings you shall take refuge;*
> *His truth shall be your shield and buckler.*
> *You shall not be afraid of the terror by night,*
> *nor of the arrow that flies by day,*

nor of the pestilence that walks in darkness,
nor of the destruction that lays waste at noonday.
A thousand may fall at your side,
and ten thousand at your right hand;
but it shall not come near you.
Only with your eyes shall you look,
and see the reward of the wicked.
Because you have made the Lord, who is my refuge,
even the Most High, your dwelling place,
no evil shall befall you,
nor shall any plague come near your dwelling;
for He shall give His angels charge over you,
to keep you in all your ways.
In their hands they shall bear you up,
lest you dash your foot against a stone.
You shall tread upon the lion and the cobra,
the young lion and the serpent you shall trample underfoot.
'Because he has set his love upon Me,
therefore I will deliver him;
I will set him on high, because he has known My name.
He shall call upon Me, and I will answer him;
I will be with him in trouble;
I will deliver him and honour him.
With long life I will satisfy him,
and show him My salvation.'"

Read it again. Dwell in the secret place! Become a Psalm 91 person! May God richly bless you!